This book belongs to:

____

Made in the USA
Las Vegas, NV
30 November 2021

35624149R00061